Made in United States
Orlando, FL
15 May 2023

33137216R00074